All mammals are born helpless, and growing to maturity is no simple task. This book is dedicated to all the family, friends, neighbors, and community members who take it upon themselves to be the village.

– Dia L. Michels

I dedicate this book to all people, young and old, who care for animals and, more generally, for nature.

– Romain Lubière

Is your child's development on track?

For checklists of all important milestones, visit CDC.gov/milestones and download the CDC's free Milestone Tracker App. For more information, call 1-800-232-4636 (agents and app available in English and Spanish).

Acting early can make a real difference!

Paperback first edition • October 2025 • ISBN: 978-1-951995-34-8
Board Book first edition • March 2026 • ISBN: 978-1-951995-36-2
eBook first edition • October 2025 • ISBN: 978-1-951995-35-5

Written by Dia L. Michels, Text © 2025
Illustrated by Romain Lubière, Illustrations © 2025

Project Manager, Cover and Book Design: Skyler Kaczmarczyk, Washington, D.C.
Editors: Hannah Thelen, Washington, D.C.
        Violet Antonick, Washington, D.C.
Editorial Assistants: Gweneth Kozlowski, Sudeeksha Dasari, and Daryn Schvimmer
Special thanks to contributor Tom Burrows.

Spanish edition coming soon.

Teacher's Guide available at the Educational Resources page of PlatypusMedia.com.

Published in the United States by:
Platypus Media, LLC
    1140 3rd Street NE
    Suite 200
    Washington, DC 20002
    (202) 546-1674
    Info@PlatypusMedia.com • PlatypusMedia.com

Distributed to the book trade by:
Baker & Taylor Publisher Services (North America)
    Toll-free: (888) 814-0208
    Orders@btpubservices.com • Btpubservices.com

Library of Congress Control Number: 2025935960

10 9 8 7 6 5 4 3 2 1

Schools, libraries, government programs, and non-profit organizations can receive bulk discounts. Contact us at the address above or email us at Info@PlatypusMedia.com

The front cover may be reproduced freely, without modification, for review or non-commercial educctional purposes.

All rights reserved. No part of this book may be reproduced in any form without the express written permission of the publisher. Front cover exempted (see above).

Printed in China.

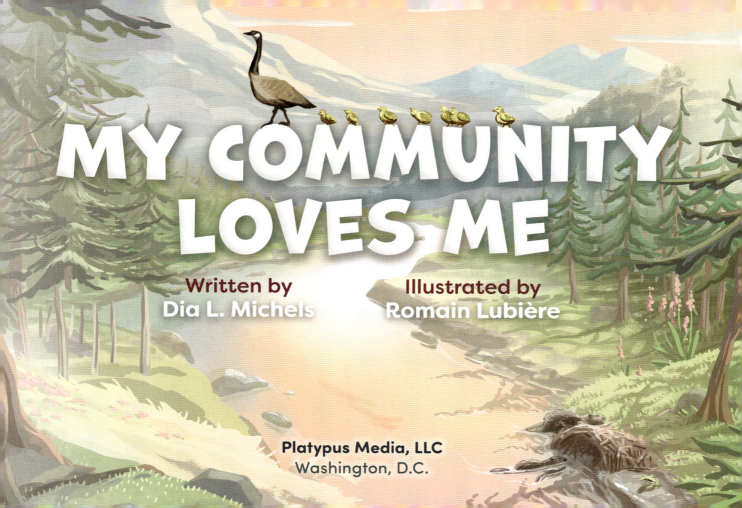

MY COMMUNITY LOVES ME

Written by
Dia L. Michels

Illustrated by
Romain Lubière

Platypus Media, LLC
Washington, D.C.

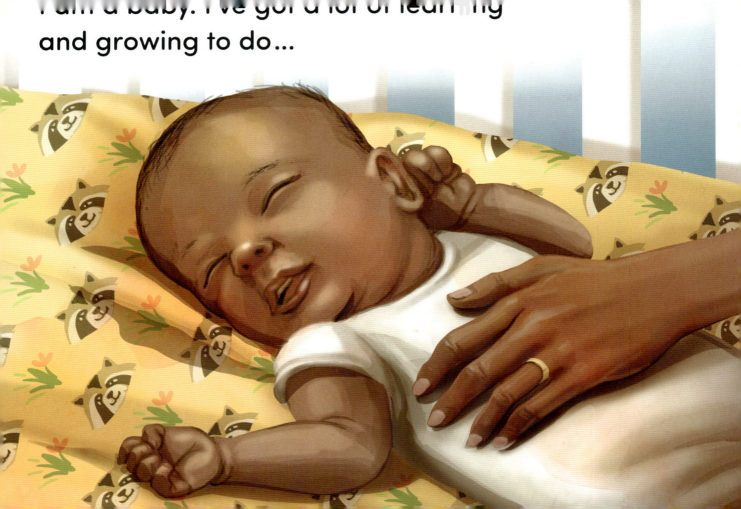

I am a baby. I've got a lot of learning and growing to do...

...so, like many baby animals, I need a lot of care from my community!

Read along to learn how you can help your baby thrive.

My community helps me feel safe and warm.

Mexican free-tailed bat pups huddle up in cozy caves while their moms fly off to snack on mosquitoes and moths. Staying close keeps them warm, safe, and tucked away until their mothers return.

Cuddle your baby to ensure they feel safe and secure.

My mom nurtures and nourishes me.

American coyote pups drink their mothers' milk when they're hungry. This yummy milk helps them grow big and strong, giving them everything they need to stay happy and healthy!

Breastfeed your baby if you can. This provides them with the perfect food for their growth and development.

My dad responds to my cries for food.

Hungry golden eaglets chirp out loud cries when their tummies are empty. Answering their calls, eagle dads swiftly swoop in with fresh fish and mice for mealtime.

Listen closely to your baby. They use different sounds to communicate what they need, from food to comfort.

My foster mom gently calls out to get my attention.

Orphaned goslings are often cared for by female Canada geese. These nurturing mothers happily welcome them into their families, honking to remind the little ones to stay close and stick together!

Talk to your baby and watch how quickly they recognize different voices and react to familiar sounds.

My siblings encourage me to eat with them.

Black-tailed jackrabbit leverets sometimes feed and rest in small groups. They nibble on delicious greens, sweet grasses, and tiny seeds, making mealtime a fun social event as they snack side by side.

Encourage your baby to self-feed with small, soft foods, when ready, to help them enjoy mealtime and develop feeding skills.

My cousins play around with me.

Brown bear cubs love to chase, wrestle, and make silly faces at each other. This playtime helps them grow stronger, grow closer, and learn important skills for growing up in the wild!

Play with your baby to strengthen your bond, help their muscles develop, and teach them important social skills.

My aunt helps me stay squeaky clean.

Western gray squirrels love to keep their little ones clean by grooming them often. This cuddly care helps the kits stay healthy and bug-free, so they can zip between trees without pesky distractions!

Clean your baby regularly with gentle baths to keep them healthy and teach the importance of good hygiene.

My grandmother shows me how to interact with others.

North American raccoon kits live in small groups where many adults help raise them. The curious kits learn by watching the grown-ups, who teach them when to purr, twitter, chitter, and squeal.

Make funny faces and sounds for your baby to imitate, helping them learn social cues and develop their own expressions.

My friends always stick by my side.

Tree frog tadpoles swim together in warm, shallow waters. While they grow, they find food and stay safe by traveling in large protective groups called shoals.

Set up playdates for your baby to help them learn how to get along with others and build lasting relationships.

My neighbors create a welcoming space for me.

Virginia opossums enjoy settling down and raising their joeys in warm burrows dug by woodchucks. When they move in, the woodchucks stay nearby, often digging a new burrow so both have their own snug homes.

Encourage your baby to share their space and toys with others to foster kindness and teamwork.

My family shows me how we care for each other.

American beaver kits stay in their colony for a few years after childhood. As they grow up, they learn to be an important part of their family, caring for new kits, gathering food, and building dams.

Motivate your growing toddler to help with chores, tidy up after themselves, and pitch in around the house.

	Litter Size (approx.)
Mountain Lion	1–4 cubs
Mexican Free-Tailed Bat	1 pup
American Coyote	4–7 pups
Golden Eagle	1–4 eaglets
Canada Geese	2–12 goslings
Black-Tailed Jackrabbit	1–8 leverets
Brown Bear	1–4 cubs
Western Gray Squirrel	3–5 kits
North American Raccoon	3–7 kits
Pacific Tree Frog	10–75 tadpoles
Virginia Opossum	7–21 joeys
American Beaver	1–4 kits

Fun Fact

Mountain lions can sleep up to 17 hours a day, taking long naps to stay rested and ready to hunt at night.

Mexican free-tailed bats can catch up to 1,000 insects in an hour, making them nature's bug-fighting superheroes!

American coyotes can leap distances of up to 12 feet (about 3.7 m), helping them escape danger and catch fast-moving prey.

Golden eagles are called raptors, like raptor dinosaurs, because their strong talons and sharp beaks help them catch prey quickly!

Canada geese can sleep with half of their brain at a time, staying alert to danger with one half, while the other half rests.

Black-tailed jackrabbits can run up to 40 miles (60 km) per hour and twist in zigzags to escape predators, staying one step ahead!

Though **brown bears'** teeth and claws make them look like meat-eaters, they mostly eat plants, spreading seeds that keep nature healthy!

Western gray squirrels build cozy stick nests for their babies in trees, and while they're away, they don't mind other squirrels using them!

Raccoons "wash" their food, but not to clean it! They dip it in water so their sensitive paws can check if it's safe to eat.

Like chameleons, **Pacific tree frogs** can change colors depending on how hot, cold, wet, or dry the air is.

Opossums are the only marsupials native to the U.S. and Canada. Like kangaroos, they carry their young in pouches.

Beavers have four front teeth that never stop growing! They shorten them by gnawing on wood while building their dams.

Dia L. Michels is an award-winning science and parenting writer of books for both children and adults. She has authored over a dozen books, many of which explore the lessons we can extract from studying mammal behaviors. A popular speaker, she presents at conferences, libraries, and schools around the country. Her books have been translated into a variety of languages. The mother of three grown children, she lives in Washington, D.C., and can be reached at Dia@PlatypusMedia.com.

Romain Lubière studied at the *École des Beaux arts* of Saint-Étienne. In 2016 he shifted his focus from graphic design to children's illustration. His portfolio offers a sensitive, poetic look at nature, the animal world, and human feelings. He combines traditional techniques (pencil, watercolor, gouache) with digital tools. He regularly offers workshops and meetings in schools, media libraries, and at book fairs. Based in Saint-Étienne, Romain continues to create and inspire from his hometown in the heart of France.

Enjoy the other books in the *Beginnings* series!

- Cuddled and Carried
- This Is How I Grow
- A Family for Zoya
- If My Mom Were a Platypus
- Babies Nurse
- …and more to come!

All titles available in Spanish and other world languages based on demand.